AF346265

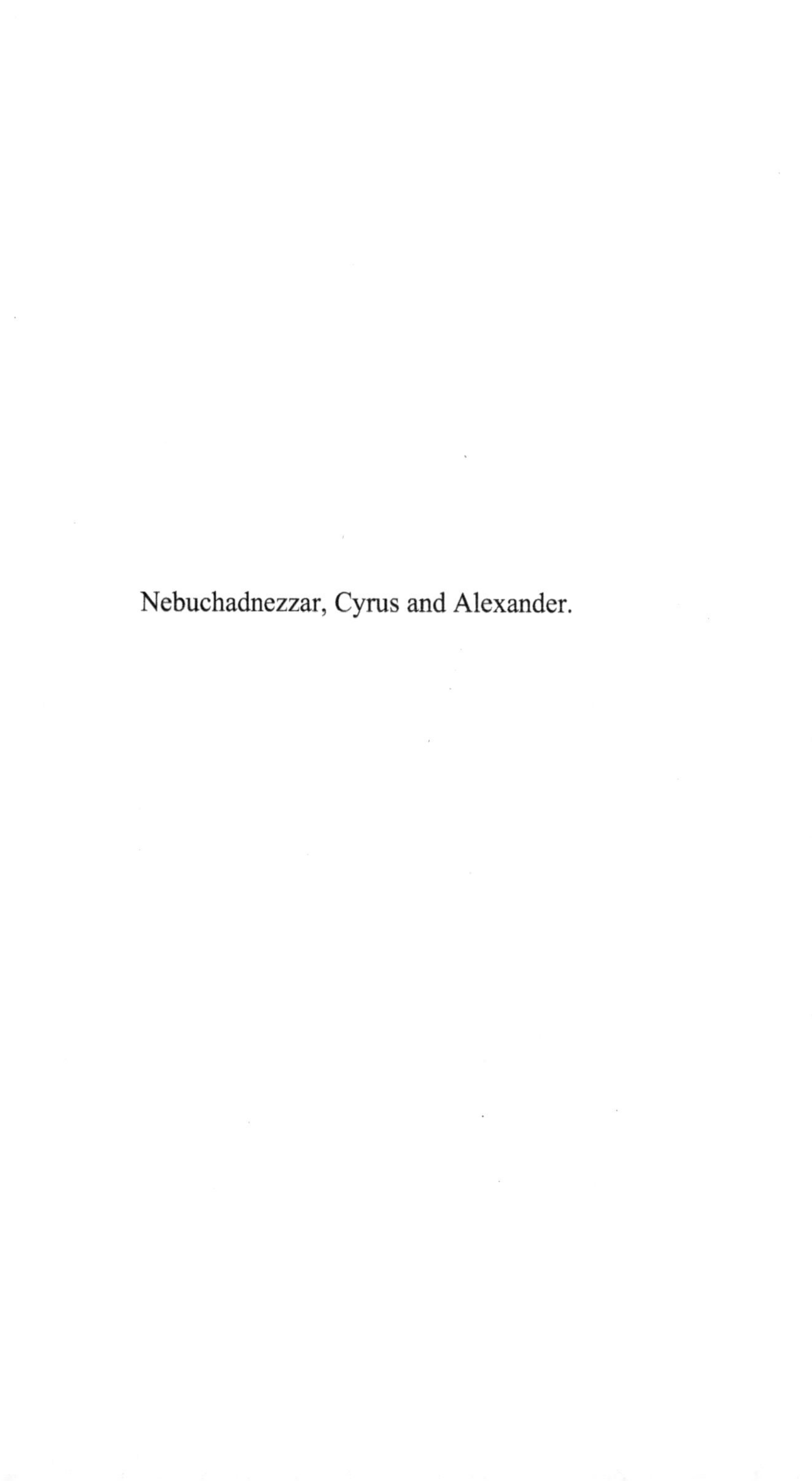

Nebuchadnezzar, Cyrus and Alexander.

Nebuchadnezzar, Cyrus and Alexander

The Great Conquerors

Collection

Nature and Human Studies

ISBN : 978-2-38469-027-5
EAN : 9782384690275

Chapter 1

Nebuchadnezzar[1]

Born about 645 B. C., and died in 561, Nebuchadnezzar was a king of Babylon, son of Nabopolassar. He rebuilt all the cities of upper Babylonia upon a magnificent scale, and embellished them with temples, palaces, aqueducts, and other public works. Early in his reign the Jews and Phœnicians rebelled. Nebuchadnezzar took Jerusalem, carried many of its chief people away captive. The book of Daniel (in the Bible) relates how he fell under the divine judgment on account of his pride, lost his reason, was deprived of his kingdom, and lived the life of a beast; and how he was restored to health and power, and acknowledged the judgment of God. It has been thought that his malady was a form of the madness called lycanthropy, in which the patient imagines himself a beast.

*

With the death of Sardanapalus, the great monarch of Assyria, and the taking of

---

[1] By Clarence Cook.

Nineveh, the capital city, by the Medes, the kingdom of Assyria came to an end, and the vast domain was parcelled out among the conquerors. At the time of the catastrophe, the district of Babylonia, with its capital city Babylon, was ruled as a dependent satrapy of Assyria by Nabopolassar. Aided by the Medes, he now took possession of the province and established himself as an independent monarch, strengthening the alliance by a marriage between the Princess Amuhia, the daughter of the Median king, and his son Nebuchadnezzar.

In the partition of Assyria, the region stretching from Egypt to the upper Euphrates, including Syria, Phœnicia, and Palestine, had fallen to the share of Nabopolassar. But the tribes that peopled it were not disposed to accept the rule of the new claimant, and looked about for an ally to support them in their resistance. Such an ally they thought they had found in Egypt.

Egypt was the great rival of Babylon, as she had been of Assyria. Both desired to control the highways of traffic connecting the Mediterranean with the farther East. Egypt had the advantage, both from her actual position on the Mediterranean and her nearer neighborhood to the coveted territory, and she used her advantage with audacity and skill. No sooner, however, did Nabopolassar feel himself firm on his throne than he resolved to check the ambition of Egypt and secure for himself the sovereignty of the lands in dispute.

The task was not an easy one. Pharaoh Necho had been for three years in possession of the whole strip along the Mediterranean— Palestine, Phœnicia, and part of Syria—and was pushing victoriously on to Assyria, when he was met at the plain of Megiddo, commanding the principal pass in the range of Mount Carmel, by the forces of the petty kingdom of Judah, disputing his advance. He defeated them in a bloody engagement, in which Josiah, King of Judah, was slain, and then continued his march to Carchemish, a stronghold built to defend one of the few fordable passes of the upper Euphrates. This important place having been taken after a bloody battle, Necho was master of all the strategic points north and west of Babylonia.

Nebuchadnezzar was now put in command of an army, to force Pharaoh to give up his prey. Marching directly upon Carchemish, he attacked the Egyptian and defeated him with great slaughter. Following up his victory, he wrested from Pharaoh, in engagement after engagement, all that he had gained in Syria, Phœnicia, and Palestine, and was in the midst of fighting in Egypt itself, when the news came of the death of his father; and he hastened home at once by forced marches to secure his possession of the throne. In his train were captives of all the nations he had conquered: Syrians, Phœnicians, Jews, and Egyptians. Among the Jewish prisoners was Daniel, the author of the book of the Old Testament called by his name, and to whom we owe the little personal knowledge we have of the great Babylonian monarch.

Of all the conquests of Nebuchadnezzar in this long struggle with Egypt, that of the Jewish people is the most interesting to us. The Jews had fought hard for independence, but if they must be conquered and held in subjection, they preferred the rule of Egypt to that of Babylon. Even the long slavery of their ancestors in that country and the sufferings it had entailed, with the tragic memories of the exodus and the wanderings in the desert, had not been potent to blot out the traditions of the years passed in that pleasant land with its delicious climate, its nourishing and abundant food. Alike in prosperity and in evil days the hearts of the people of Israel yearned after Egypt, and the denunciations of her prophets are never so bitter as when uttered against those who turned from Jehovah to worship the false gods of the Nile. Three times did the inhabitants of Jerusalem rebel against the rule of Babylon, and three times did Nebuchadnezzar come down upon them with a cruel and unrelenting vengeance, carrying off their people into bondage, each time inflicting great damage upon the city and leaving her less capable of resistance; yet each time her rulers had turned to Egypt in the vain hope of finding in her a defence against the oppressor, but in every instance Egypt had proved a broken reed.

Of the three successive kings of Judah whom Nebuchadnezzar had left to rule the city as his servants, and who had all in turn rebelled against him, one had been condemned to perpetual imprisonment in Babylon; a second had been carried there in chains and probably killed, while the third, captured in a vain attempt to escape after the taking of the city, had first been made to see his sons killed before his eyes, had then been cruelly blinded, and afterward carried in chains to Babylon, and cast into prison. The last siege of the city lasted eighteen months, and when it was finally taken by assault, its ruin was complete. By previous deportations Jerusalem had been deprived of her princes, her warriors, her craftsmen, and her smiths, with all the treasure laid up in the palace of her kings, and all the vessels of gold and silver consecrated to the worship of Jehovah. Little then was left for her to suffer, when the punishment of her latest rebellion came. Her walls were thrown down, her temple, her chief glory, was destroyed, the greater part of the inhabitants who had survived the prolonged siege were carried off to swell the crowd of exiles already in Babylon, and only a few of the humbler sort of folk, the vine-dressers and the small farmers, were left behind.

When Nebuchadnezzar rested after his conquests, secure in the subjugation of his rivals, and in the possession of his vast kingdom, he gave himself up to the material improvement of Babylon and the surrounding country.

The city as he left it, at the end of his reign of forty-three years, was built on both sides of the Euphrates, and covered a space of four hundred square miles, equal to five times the size of London. It was surrounded by a triple wall of brick; the innermost, over three hundred feet high, and eighty-five feet broad at the top, with room for four chariots to drive abreast. The walls were pierced by one hundred gate-ways framed in brass and with brazen gates, and at the points where the Euphrates entered and left the city the walls also turned and followed the course of the river, thus dividing the city into two fortified parts. These two districts were connected by a bridge of stone piers, guarded by portcullises, and ferries also plied between the quays that lined the river-banks, to which access was given by gates in the walls.

Nebuchadnezzar's palace was a splendid structure covering a large space at one end of the bridge. In the central court were the Hanging Gardens, the chief glory of the city, and reckoned one of the wonders of the world. No clear idea can be formed of these gardens from any description that has come down to us, but it would appear that arches eighty feet high supported terraces of earth planted with all the skill for which the gardeners of the East were famous. We are told that they were built for the pleasure of Queen Amuhia, who, as a Median princess, missed her native mountains, but a more commonplace explanation is that they were carried so high to escape the mosquitoes that swarmed on the lower level.

Various splendid edifices, chiefly religious, adorned the great squares of the city: the temple of the god Bel, enriched by the spoils of Tyre and Jerusalem, was the especial pride of Nebuchadnezzar. It rose in a succession of eight lofty stages, and supported on the top a golden statue of the god, forty feet high. Still another temple of Bel was built in seven stages, each faced with enamelled brick of one of the planetary colors; the topmost one of blue, the color dedicated to Mercury or Nebo, the patron god of Nabopolassar.

But the most important of the civic undertakings of Nebuchadnezzar was the extension of the great system of canalization by which the barren wastes of the Babylonian plain were made to rival the valley of the Nile in fertility, and become the granary of the East. The whole territory was covered with a network of canals fed by the

Tigris and Euphrates, and used for both irrigation and navigation. One branch had already connected Nineveh with Babylon, and another constructed by Nebuchadnezzar united Babylon to the Persian Gulf, running a distance of four hundred miles. This is still to be traced in a portion of its length.

*

The fate of Nebuchadnezzar is one of the most tragic in the long list of calamities that have overtaken the great and powerful of the earth.

According to Daniel, it was just after the king had spoken those words of exulting pride as he walked in the palace of the Kingdom of Babylon: "Is not this great Babylon that I have built," when he was attacked by that dreadful form of madness, called by the Greeks, lycanthropy (wolf-man), in which the victim fancies himself a beast: in its fiercer manifestations a beast of the forest, or in milder visitations a beast of the field.

Nebuchadnezzar's madness became so violent that for four years he was exiled from his throne and from the company of men, and wandered in the fields, eating grass like oxen, "and his body was wet with the dews of heaven, and his hairs were grown like eagles' feathers, and his nails like birds' claws." Although no mention is made of this strange malady in any writing but the book of Daniel, yet it has a pathetic confirmation in one of the rock-cut inscriptions that record the acts of Nebuchadnezzar's reign. "For four years the seat of my kingdom did not rejoice my heart. In all my dominions I built no high place of power, nor did I lay up the precious treasure of my kingdom. In Babylon I erected no buildings for myself nor for the glory of my empire. In the worship of Bel-

Merodach, my Lord, the joy of my heart, in Babylon the city of his worship and the seat of my empire, I did not sing his praise, nor did I furnish his altar with victims"—and then, as if returning to the thing that lay nearest him—"In four years I did not dig out the canals."

In time, the black cloud of the king's madness passed away and health and reason were restored to him. And if the words that Daniel puts into the king's mouth on his recovery are really his, we must recognize in this Eastern Despot a decided strain of religious sensibility, a trait that appears beside in his almost passionate expressions of affection for his god Merodach, and in his sympathy with Daniel and the youths who were his companions, in their own religious devotion.

Although Daniel and the other youths whom the king had caused to be called out from the mass of the Jewish captives for his own particular service — boys distinguished from the rest by their personal beauty, their intelligence and aptitude — were too earnest in their religious convictions and too high-spirited to conform to the Babylonian religion or to conceal their sentiments under the cloak of policy, yet the king tolerated their adherence to their ritual and yielded only in part to the persistence of the Jew-baiters, who saw with angry eyes the promotion of the hated captives to places of power and authority over the heads of their captors. In spite of his enemies Daniel was allowed to exercise his own religion in peace; and the persecutors of his companions, Shadrach, Meshach, and Abednego, were themselves destroyed in the furnace they had heated for their innocent victims, which the youths themselves were rescued from by the personal interposition of the king, who pretended to see — or in his religious exaltation did really see — the god himself standing guard over the victims in the midst of the flames.

Of Nebuchadnezzar after the recovery of his reason we learn but little. The chronicle of Daniel passes abruptly from Nebuchadnezzar to Belshazzar, and the great king is not mentioned again. History, too, is silent. It tells us only that he left the throne to a son, whose name, Evil-Merodach, records the devotion of his father to the god of his people.

Nebuchadnezzar and the History of
Babylonian Empire.[2]

Babylon was the capital city of the Babylonian Empire considered as the third great empire of the history after Egypt and Assyria. The name Babylon is the Greek form of Babel or Bab-ili, "the gate of the god", which again is the Semitic translation of the original Sumerian name Ka-dimirra.

The claim to supremacy of Babylon in Asia, however real in fact, was not admitted until the claimant had "taken the hands" of Bel-Merodach at Babylon, and thereby been accepted as his adopted son and the inheritor of the old Babylonian empire. It was this which made Tiglath-pileser III and other Assyrian kings so anxious to possess themselves of Babylon and so to legitimize

---

[2] cf *Babylon*, by A Henry Sayce.

their power. Sennacherib alone seems to have failed in securing the support of the Babylonian priesthood; at all events he never underwent the ceremony, and Babylonia throughout his reign was in a constant state of revolt which was finally suppressed only by the complete destruction of the capital. In 689 B.C. its walls, temples and palaces were razed to the ground and the rubbish thrown into the Arakhtu, the canal which bordered the earlier Babylon on the south. The act shocked the religious conscience of western Asia; the subsequent murder of Sennacherib was held to be an expiation of it, and his successor Esar-haddon hastened to rebuild the old city, to receive there his crown, and make it his residence during part of the year. On his death Babylonia was left to his elder son Samas-sum-yukin, who eventually headed a revolt against his brother Assur-bani-pal of Assyria. Once more Babylon was besieged by the Assyrians and starved into surrender. Assur-bani-pal purified the city and celebrated a "service of reconciliation," but did not venture to "take the hands" of Bel.

In the subsequent overthrow of the Assyrian empire the Babylonians saw another example of divine vengeance.

With the recovery of Babylonian independence under Nabopolassar a new era of architectural activity set in, and his son Nebuchadrezzar made Babylon one of the wonders of the ancient world. It surrendered without a struggle to Cyrus, but two sieges in the reign of Darius Hystaspis, and one in the reign of Xerxes, brought about the destruction of the defences, while the monotheistic rule of Persia allowed the temples to fall into decay. Indeed part of the temple of E-Saggila, which like other ancient temples served as a fortress, was intentionally pulled down by Xerxes after his capture of the city. Alexander was murdered in the palace of Nebuchadrezzar, which must therefore have been still standing, and cuneiform texts show that, even under the Seleucids, E-Saggila was not wholly a ruin. The foundation of Seleucia in its neighbourhood, however, drew away the population of the old city and hastened its material decay. A tablet dated 275 B.C. states that on the 12th of Nisan the inhabitants of Babylon were transported to the new town, where a palace was built as well as a temple to which the ancient name of E-Saggila was given. With this event the history of Babylon comes practically to an end, though more than a century later we find sacrifices being still performed in its old sanctuary.

Our knowledge of its topography is derived from the classical writers, the inscriptions of Nebuchadrezzar, and the excavations of the *Deutsche Orientgesellschaft*, which were begun in 1899. The topography is necessarily that of the Babylon of Nebuchadrezzar; the older Babylon which was destroyed by Sennacherib having left few, if any, traces behind. Most of the existing remains lie on the E. bank of the Euphrates, the principal being three vast mounds, the *Babil* to the north, the *Qasr* or "Palace" (also known as the *Mujelliba*) in the centre, and the Ishān ʿAmrān ibn ʿAli, with the outlying spur of the Jumjuma, to the south. Eastward of these come the Ishān el-Aswad or "Black Mound" and three lines of rampart, one of which encloses the *Babil* mound on the N. and E. sides, while a third forms a triangle with the S.E. angle of the other two. W. of the Euphrates are other ramparts and the remains of the ancient Borsippa.

We learn from Herodotus and Ctesias that the city was built on both sides of the river in the form of a square, and enclosed within a double row of lofty walls to which Ctesias adds a third. Ctesias makes the outermost wall 360 stades (42 m.) in circumference, while according to Herodotus it measured 480 stades (56 m.), which would include an area of about 200 sq. m. The estimate of Ctesias is essentially the same as that of Q. Curtius (v. 1. 26), 368 stades, and Clitarchus (*ap.* Diod. Sic. ii. 7), 365 stades; Strabo (xvi. 1. 5) makes it 385 stades. But even the estimate of Ctesias, assuming the stade to be its usual length, would imply an area of about 100 sq. m. According to Herodotus the height of the walls was about 335 ft. and their width 85 ft; according to Ctesias the height was about 300 ft. The measurements seem exaggerated, but we must remember that even in Xenophon's time (*Anab.* iii. 4.

10) the ruined wall of Nineveh was still 150 ft high, and that the spaces between the 250 towers of the wall of Babylon (Ctes. 417, *ap.* Diod. ii. 7) were broad enough to let a four-horse chariot turn (Herod. i. 179). The clay dug from the moat served to make the bricks of the wall, which had 100 gates, all of bronze, with bronze lintels and posts. The two inner enclosures were faced with enamelled tiles and represented hunting-scenes. Two other walls ran along the banks of the Euphrates and the quays with which it was lined, each containing 25 gates which answered to the number of streets they led into. Ferry-boats plied between the landing-places of the gates, and a movable drawbridge (30 ft. broad), supported on stone piers, joined the two parts of the city together.

The account thus given of the walls must be grossly exaggerated and cannot have been that of an eye-witness. Moreover, the two walls — Imgur-Bel, the inner wall, and Nimitti-Bel, the outer — which enclosed the city proper on the site of the older Babylon have been confused with the outer ramparts (enclosing the whole of Nebuchadrezzar's city), the remains of which can still be traced to the east.

According to Nebuchadrezzar, Imgur-Bel was built in the form of a square, each side of which measured "30 *aslu* by the great cubit"; this would be equivalent, if Professor F. Hommel is right, to 2400 metres. Four thousand cubits to the east the great rampart was built "mountain high," which surrounded both the old and the new town; it was provided with a moat, and a reservoir was excavated in the triangle on the inner side of its south-east corner, the western wall of which is still visible. The Imgur-Bel of Sargon's time has been discovered by the

German excavators running south of the *Qasr* from the Euphrates to the Gate of Ishtar.

The German excavations have shown that the *Qasr* mound represents both the old palace of Nabopolassar, and the new palace adjoining it built by Nebuchadrezzar, the wall of which he boasts of having completed in 15 days. They have also laid bare the site of the "Gate of Ishtar" on the east side of the mound and the little temple of Nin-Makh (Beltis) beyond it, as well as the raised road for solemn processions (*A-ibur-sabu*) which led from the Gate of Ishtar to E-Saggila and skirted the east side of the palace. The road was paved with stone and its walls on either side lined with enamelled tiles, on which a procession of lions is represented. North of the mound was a canal, which seems to have been the Libilkhegal of the inscriptions, while on the south side was the Arakhtu, "the river of Babylon," the brick quays of which were built by Nabopolassar.

The site of E-Saggila is still uncertain. The German excavators assign it to the ʿAmrān mound, its tower having stood in a depression immediately to the north of this, and so place it south of the *Qasr*; but E. Lindl and F. Hommel have put forward strong reasons for considering it to have been north of the latter, on a part of the site which has not yet been explored. A tablet copied by George Smith gives us interesting details as to the plan and dimensions of this famous temple of Bel; a plan based on these will be found in Hommel's *Grundriss der Geographie und Geschichte des alten Orients*, p. 321. There were three courts, the outer or great court, the middle court of Ishtar and Zamama, and the inner court on the east side of which was the tower of seven stages (known as the House of the

Foundation of Heaven and Earth), 90 metres high according to Hommel's calculation of the measurements in the tablet; while on the west side was the temple proper of Merodach and his wife Sarpanit or Zarpanit, as well as chapels of Anu, Ea and Bel on either side of it. A winding ascent led to the summit of the tower, where there was a chapel, containing, according to Herodotus, a couch and golden table (for the showbread) but no image. The golden image of Merodach 40 ft. high, stood in the temple below, in the sanctuary called E-Kua or "House of the Oracle," together with a table, a mercy-seat and an altar — all of gold. The deities whose chapels were erected within the precincts of the temple enclosure were regarded as forming his court. Fifty-five of these chapels existed altogether in Babylon, but some of them stood independently in other parts of the city.

There are numerous gates in the walls both of E-Saggila and of the city, the names of many of which are now known. Nebuchadrezzar says that he covered the walls of some of them with blue enamelled tiles "on which bulls and dragons were pourtrayed," and that he set up large bulls and serpents of bronze on their thresholds.

The *Babil* mound probably represents the site of a palace built by Nebuchadrezzar at the northern extremity of the city walls and attached to a defensive outwork 60 cubits in length. Since H. Rassam found remains of irrigation works here it might well be the site of the Hanging Gardens. These consisted, we are told, of a garden of trees and flowers, built on the topmost of a series of arches some 75 ft. high, and in the form of a square, each side of which measured 400 Greek ft. Water was raised from the Euphrates by means of a screw). In the Jumjuma mound at the southern extremity of the old city the contract and other business tablets of the Egibi firm were found.

Chapter 2

Cyrus the Great[3]

Cyrus was the founder of the ancient Persian Empire, a monarchy, perhaps, the most wealthy and magnificent which the world has ever seen. Of that strange and incomprehensible principle of human nature, under the influence of which vast masses of men, notwithstanding the universal instinct of aversion to control, combine, under certain circumstances, by millions and millions, to maintain, for many successive centuries, the representatives of some one great family in a condition of exalted, and absolute, and utterly irresponsible ascendency over themselves, while they toil for them, watch over them, submit to endless and most humiliating privations in their behalf, and commit, if commanded to do so, the most inexcusable and atrocious crimes to sustain the demigods they have thus made in their lofty estate, we have, in the case of this Persian monarchy, one of the most extraordinary exhibitions.

*

---

[3] By Clarence Cook

The early life of Cyrus the Persian, like that of many another famous conqueror, is lost in a cloud of fable. According to Herodotus, to whom we owe the earliest account, Astyages the King of Media was warned in a dream that some danger threatened the kingdom from the offspring of his daughter Mandane, who as yet was unmarried. In order to remove the danger, whatever it might be, as far as possible from his throne, Astyages married his daughter to a Persian named Cambyses, who took her with him to his own country. But after his daughter's marriage Astyages had another dream, which was interpreted by the priests to mean that his daughter's child was destined to reign in his stead. Alarmed by this prophecy he sent for his daughter, and when in course of time she bore a son, he ordered his trusty lieutenant Harpagus to carry the child to his own house and kill it.

Harpagus took the infant as he had been ordered to do, but moved by the pleadings of his wife he determined to commit the rest of his bloody instructions to other hands. He therefore called one of his herdsmen, and ordered him to expose the child on the bleakest part of the mountain and leave it to perish, threatening him with the most terrible penalties in case of disobedience. But the herdsman and his wife were no more proof against pity than Harpagus and his wife had been, and while they stood swayed between their wish to save the child and their fear of disobeying Harpagus, fortune happily provided an escape for them.

The wife of the herdsman brought forth a dead child, and this they determined to substitute for the living infant, and to bring up the grandson of Astyages as their own. The exchange was accomplished, and after some days the servants of Harpagus, sent to inquire if their master's commands had been obeyed, were shown by the herdsman the body of a dead child exposed on the rocks and still wearing the rich clothes and ornaments in which it had been brought to his house. Harpagus was thus enabled to assure Astyages that he was safe from the threatened danger, and might enjoy his throne in peace.

When the child of Mandane was ten years old an accident brought him to the knowledge of the king, and restored him to his birthright. One day he was playing with the children of his neighbors, and in a certain game where it was necessary to make one of the players king, Cyrus was chosen, and all the others, as his subjects, promised to obey his commands. But one of the boys, the son of a rich noble of the court of Astyages, refused to do as he was bid by Cyrus, and according to the rule of the game, he had to submit to a beating at the hand of the boy-king. Angry at this treatment, he complained to his father, who, indignant in his turn, went to Astyages, and reproached him with the blows his son had received at the hands of the son of one of the king's slaves. Cyrus was brought before the king; but when he was asked how he had dared to treat the son of a nobleman in such a way, the boy, nothing daunted, answered that he had done only what was right: the rules of the game were known to all who had joined in it: the other boys had submitted to the penalties: the son of the nobleman alone had refused, and he had been punished as he deserved. "If any wrong has been done by me," he said, "I am ready to suffer for it." Struck by the boldness of the lad, and by something in his looks, Astyages dismissed him for a time, and promised the nobleman that he should be satisfied for the insults offered to his son. He then sent for the herdsman Mitridates and wrung from him a confession of what he had done; and learning how Harpagus had deceived him he acquitted Mitridates, and turned all his vengeance upon Harpagus as the chief offender. How cruelly he punished him must not be told here, for pity, but it was such a barbarous revenge as could never be forgiven; and though Harpagus pretended to make light of it, yet it was only that by keeping fair with the king he might bide his time, and repay cruelty with cruelty.

But now, as Cyrus in our story has grown to man's estate, and is ready to show the world of what stuff he is made, it will be well to explain in a few words, what was the state of things in that part of the world where he was to play his part.

Cyrus the Great

The mighty Kingdom of Assyria in its greatest estate had stretched from the Indus on the east, to the Mediterranean on the west. But when Nineveh, the capital and chief city of the empire, had been destroyed by the Medes—a subject people living on the north-eastern borders of the kingdom, but who had risen in rebellion against their rulers—Assyria was broken in pieces, and several minor kingdoms rose on her ruins.

Of these the chief were Media and Babylonia in the east, and Lydia in the west. Babylonia rose to a great height of power and splendor under Nebuchadnezzar, as we have seen in our sketch of that king's life. The Medes, a brave and warlike people, never attained to so high a degree of civilization as the Babylonians, nor did they ever have a monarch whose fame equalled that of Sardanapalus, the King of Assyria; of Nebuchadnezzar; or of Crœsus, King of Lydia; but under a succession of astute and hardy warriors, who held the throne for something over one hundred and fifty years, their dominion was gradually extended until it stretched from the Indus to the centre of Asia Minor. Their greatest achievement had been the destruction of Nineveh in B.C. 606.

Lydia, the remaining province, touched the Median kingdom on the east, and on the west was only separated, in the beginning, from the Mediterranean by the narrow strip of territory occupied by the Greek colonies, which for a time acted as a bar to the encroachments of the Lydian monarchs and their conquerors.

When Cyrus came to manhood, these kingdoms, the successors of the Assyrian monarchy, were all flourishing in wealth and power. Media was ruled by Astyages, his grandfather—to accept the legendary history as it has come down to us; Babylonia the greatest of the three was governed by Nebuchadnezzar, while Lydia was ruled by Crœsus, a monarch wise above his peers, whose name has long been a synonym for unbounded wealth, and whose story, though not beyond the bounds of credibility, reads more like a fable of romance than a tale of sober fact.

Crœsus was the brother-in-law of Astyages, and in close alliance not only with the Medes, but with the Babylonians, the Egyptians, and the Greeks; and he was at the height of his power and was looking forward to still greater increase of his dominions, when in an evil hour he struck against the growing greatness of Cyrus, and was crushed in the encounter. Had he been less arrogant, the doom he wrought for himself might have been delayed, but it could not have been wholly averted. Nothing could have long withstood the greed of Cyrus for universal dominion.

We have seen what good cause Harpagus had to hate Astyages. But he nursed his revenge with crafty wisdom, and knowing himself powerless to act openly and alone, he tried what stratagem might do to bring about his aim, which was no less than the overthrow of Astyages by means of the tyrant's grandson, Cyrus. He did not take open measures until he knew he had allies enough at his back, and could strike with a sure aim. He worked with the great Median chiefs in private, stirring them up against Astyages by appeals of all sorts: to their ambition, their greed, their discontent, their private wrongs; and when he had secured the consent of enough nobles to his plans, he called upon Cyrus, as one who had chiefly suffered from the tyranny and cruelty of the king, to lead the proposed revolt in person. He knew that Cyrus had been gradually strengthening his own kingdom of Persia in preparation for the ambitious schemes of conquest he was nursing, but there was danger in correspondence with one who stood to Astyages in the double relation of a feared and hated grandson, and the chief of a rival people; and if we may believe Herodotus, Harpagus had recourse to a strange expedient to communicate his design to Cyrus. Disembowelling a dead hare, he inserted a letter in the cavity, and sent the animal to Cyrus as a present.

When the letter came to the hands of Cyrus he eagerly accepted the offers it contained of leadership in the proposed revolt, and joined his forces with those of the disaffected Medes. Astyages was overthrown and his kingdom taken possession of by Cyrus. Herodotus draws a striking picture of the exultation of Harpagus over the success of his revengeful projects, and of the disdain with which Astyages reproached him for having called on another to do what, trusted and confided in as he was by his monarch, he might have accomplished for himself, and reaped the harvest which he had surrendered to another. Cyrus had the wisdom to spare the life of Astyages, and to attach him to his person as councillor and friend. Harpagus he made his lieutenant, and much of his success was owing to this man's wisdom and bravery. After the defeat of Astyages, Cyrus advanced against the lesser tribes that had owed allegiance to the Median king, and having reduced them one by one to submission, the power of the once mighty empire of the Medians passed to the inheritance of the Persians in the year 559 B.C.

When Crœsus heard of the overthrow of his brother-in-law by the hands of Cyrus, and of the setting up a great new monarchy on the ruins of the fallen kingdom, his own ambitious projects were blown into fresh activity by the desire for private revenge. Misled by his own interpretation of the oracle he consulted as to the likelihood of success in an expedition against the Persians, he advanced to withstand the conquering march of Cyrus; and his first success was against the Syrians of Cappadocia, a people subject to Cyrus, as having formed a part of the Median Kingdom. Cyrus, with a powerful army, came at once to the assistance of his new subjects, and meeting the forces of Crœsus on the plain of Cappadocia, a fiercely fought, but indecisive battle took place, which resulted in the retreat of Crœsus to his capital, Sardis, to seek the assistance of his allies and prepare to meet Cyrus with a larger force. In overweening confidence in his own success, he dismissed his mercenary troops, and sent messengers to Babylon, to Egypt, and to Sparta, calling on them to come with troops to his assistance within five months. No sooner had he shut himself up in Sardis, and dismissed his mercenaries, depending upon his own forces until assistance should come from his allies, than Cyrus advanced against him so swiftly that there was no escape from a battle.

Crœsus, believing in his fortune, and trusting to the excellence of his cavalry, boldly took the field; but Cyrus, using stratagem where perhaps courage would not have availed, put his camels in front of his line, and massed his own horsemen behind them. The horses of Crœsus, maddened by the unaccustomed smell of the camels, refused to advance; but the Lydians, dismounting, fought so bravely on foot with their spears, that it was not until after a long and fierce combat that they were forced to retreat and seek safety within the walls of Sardis.

The army of Cyrus invested the city, but it was so strongly fortified on all sides but one as to be impregnable by assault and the side left unprotected by art was supposed to be amply protected by nature, since it abutted on the very edge of a steep precipice. But, after the siege had lasted fourteen days, a Persian sentinel saw one of the garrison descend the precipice to recover his helmet that had rolled down; and no sooner had he thus unwittingly showed the way, than the sentinel followed with a number of his fellow-soldiers and, reaching the top of the cliff in safety, attacked the guards, all unsuspicious, and gained an entrance to the city. The gates were opened to the Persians, and Crœsus with all his vast store of treasure became the prey of the conqueror. The fall of Sardis and the Lydian monarchy was followed by the subjection of the Greek cities of Asia Minor, a task which Cyrus left to the hands of Harpagus, while he himself turned eastward to pursue his conquests in Upper Asia and in Assyria. His greatest achievement in this quarter was the taking of

Babylon. This he accomplished in the reign of Belshazzar, one of the successors of Nebuchadnezzar, perhaps his son, by turning the Euphrates, which ran through the middle of the city, out of its course; and when its bed was dry he entered the city by this road and captured it with little resistance.

Cyrus was now the sole master of the vast Assyrian Kingdom, once more in his hands brought back to something like the unity it had before the great Median revolt. But he was not content, nor was it perhaps possible for him to rest in the enjoyment of power and possessions extorted by force, and dependent on force to hold. The new empire, like the old one, was destined to break in pieces by its own weight. Cyrus was kept in constant activity by the necessity of resisting the inroads on his empire of the tribes in the north and farther east; and it was in endeavoring to repel invasion and to maintain order in the regions he had already conquered, that he met his death. After a reign of thirty years he was slain, in 529 B.C., in battle with the Massagetæ, a tribe of Central Asia. He left his kingdom to his son Cambyses.

Cyrus and his Conquests[4].

That Cyrus was the first Persian conqueror, and that the space which he overran covered no less than fifty degrees of longitude, from the coast of Asia Minor to the Oxus and the Indus, are facts quite indisputable. The native Persians, whom he conducted to an empire so immense, were an aggregate of seven agricultural, and four nomadic tribes — all of them rude, hardy, and brave — dwelling in a mountainous region, clothed in skins, ignorant of wine, or fruit, or any of the commonest luxuries of life, and despising the very idea of purchase or sale. Their tribes were very unequal in point of dignity, probably also in respect to

---

[4] cf George Grote, *The Conquests of Cyrus the Great.*

numbers and powers, among one another. First in estimation among them stood the Pasargadæ; and the first phratry or clan among the Pasargadæ were the Achæmenidæ, to whom Cyrus himself belonged. Whether his relationship to the Median king whom he dethroned was a matter of fact, or a politic fiction, we cannot well determine. But Xenophon, in noticing the spacious deserted cities, Larissa and Mespila, which he saw in his march with the ten thousand Greeks on the eastern side of the Tigris, gives us to understand that the conquest of Media by the Persians was reported to him as having been an obstinate and protracted struggle. However this may be, the preponderance of the Persians was at last complete: though the Medes always continued to be the second nation in the empire, after the Persians, properly so called; and by early Greek writers the great enemy in the East is often called "the Mede" as well as "the Persian." The Median Ekbatana too remained as one of the capital cities, and the usual summer residence, of the kings of Persia; Susa on the Choaspes, on the Kissian plain farther southward, and east of the Tigris, being their winter abode.

*

The vast space of country comprised between the Indus on the east, the Oxus and Caspian Sea to the north, the Persian Gulf and Indian Ocean to the south, and the line of Mount Zagros to the west, appears to have been occupied in these times by a great variety of different tribes and people, yet all or most of them belonging to the religion of Zoroaster, and speaking dialects of the Zend language. It was known amongst its inhabitants by the common name of Iran or Aria: it is, in its central parts at least, a high, cold plateau, totally destitute of wood, and scantily supplied with water; much of it indeed is a salt and sandy desert, unsusceptible of culture. Parts of it are eminently fertile, where water can be procured and irrigation applied. Scattered masses of tolerably dense population thus grew up; but continuity of cultivation is not practicable, and in ancient times, as at present, a large proportion of the population of Iran seems to have consisted of wandering or nomadic tribes with their tents and cattle. The rich pastures, and the freshness of the summer climate, in the region of mountain and valley near Ekbatana, are extolled by modern travellers, just as they attracted the

Great King in ancient times during the hot months. The more southerly province called Persis proper (Faristan) consists also in part of mountain land interspersed with valley and plain, abundantly watered, and ample in pasture, sloping gradually down to low grounds on the sea-coast which are hot and dry: the care bestowed both by Medes and Persians on the breeding of their horses was remarkable. There were doubtless material differences between different parts of the population of this vast plateau of Iran. Yet it seems that, along with their common language and religion, they had also something of a common character, which contrasted with the Indian population east of the Indus, the Assyrians west of Mount Zagros, and the Massagetæ and other Nomads of the Caspian and the Sea of

Aral—less brutish, restless and blood-thirsty than the latter—more fierce, contemptuous and extortionate, and less capable of sustained industry, than the two former. There can be little doubt, at the time of which we are now speaking, when the wealth and cultivation of Assyria were at their maximum, that Iran also was far better peopled than ever it has been since European observers have been able to survey it—especially the north-eastern portion, Bactria and Sogdiana—so that the invasions of the Nomads from Turkestan and Tartary, which have been so destructive at various intervals since the Mohammedan conquest, were before that period successfully kept back.

The general analogy among the population of Iran probably enabled the Persian conqueror with comparative ease to extend his empire to the east, after the conquest of Ekbatana, and to become the full heir of the Median kings. If we may believe Ctesias, even the distant province of Bactria had been before subject to those kings. At first it resisted Cyrus, but finding that he had become son-in-law of Astyages, as well as master of his person, it speedily acknowledged his authority.

According to the representation of Herodotus, the war between Cyrus and Croesus of Lydia began shortly after the capture of Astyages, and before the conquest of Bactria. Croesus was the assailant, wishing to avenge his brother-in-law, to arrest the growth of the Persian conqueror, and to increase his own dominions. His more prudent counsellors in vain represented to him that he had little to gain, and much to lose, by war with a nation alike hardy and poor. He is represented as just at that time recovering from the affliction arising out of the death of his son.

To ask advice of the oracle, before he took any final decision, was a step which no pious king would omit. But in the present perilous question, Croesus did more—he took a precaution so extreme, that if his piety had not been placed beyond all doubt by his extraordinary munificence to the temples, he might have drawn upon himself the suspicion of a guilty scepticism. Before he would send to ask advice respecting the project itself, he resolved to test the credit of some of the chief surrounding oracles— Delphi, Dodona, Branchidæ near Miletus, Amphiaraus at Thebes, Trophonius at

Labadeia, and Ammon in Libya. His envoys started from Sardis on the same day, and were all directed on the hundredth day afterward to ask at the respective oracles how Croesus was at that precise moment employed. This was a severe trial: of the manner in which it was met by four out of the six oracles consulted we have no information, and it rather appears that their answers were unsatisfactory. But Amphiaraus maintained his credit undiminished, while Apollo at Delphi, more omniscient than Apollo at Branchidæ, solved the question with such unerring precision, as to afford a strong additional argument against persons who might be disposed to scoff at divination. No sooner had the envoys put the question to the Delphian priestess, on the day named, "What is Croesus now doing?" than she exclaimed in the accustomed hexameter verse, "I know the number of grains of sand, and the measures of the sea: I understand the dumb, and I hear the man who speaks not. The smell reaches me of a hard-skinned tortoise boiled in a copper with lamb's flesh—copper above and copper below." Croesus was awe-struck on receiving this reply. It described with the utmost detail that which he had been really doing, so that he accounted the Delphian oracle and that of Amphiaraus the only trustworthy oracles on earth—following up these feelings with a holocaust of the most munificent character, in order to win the favor of the Delphian god. Three thousand cattle were offered up, and upon a vast sacrificial pile were placed the most splendid purple robes and tunics, together with couches and censers of gold and silver; besides which he sent to Delphi itself the richest presents in gold and silver—statues, bowls, jugs, etc., the size and weight of which we read with astonishment; the more so as Herodotus himself saw them a century afterwards at Delphi. Nor was Croesus altogether unmindful of Amphiaraus, whose answer had been creditable, though less triumphant than that of the Pythian priestess. He sent to Amphiaraus a spear and shield of pure gold, which were afterward seen at Thebes by Herodotus: this large donative may help the reader to conceive the immensity of those which he sent to Delphi.

The envoys who conveyed these gifts were instructed to ask at the same time, whether Croesus should undertake an expedition against the Persians—and if so, whether he should solicit any allies to assist him. In regard to the second question, the answer both of Apollo and of Amphiaraus was deci sive, recommending him to invite the alliance of the most powerful Greeks. In regard to the first and most momentous question, their answer was as remarkable for circumspection as it had been before for detective sagacity: they told Croesus that if he invaded the Persians, he would subvert a mighty monarchy. The blindness of Croesus interpreted this declaration into an unqualified promise of success: he sent further presents to the oracle, and again inquired whether his kingdom would be durable. "When a mule shall become king of the Medes (replied the priestess) then must thou run away—be not ashamed."

More assured than ever by such an answer, Croesus sent to Sparta, under the kings Anaxandrides and Aristo, to tender presents and solicit their alliance. His propositions were favorably entertained—the more so, as he had before gratuitously furnished some gold to the Lacedæmonians for a statue to Apollo. The alliance now formed was altogether general—no express effort being as yet demanded from them, though it soon came to be. But the incident is to be noted, as marking the first plunge of the leading Grecian state into Asiatic politics; and that too without any of the generous Hellenic sympathy which afterward induced Athens to send her citizens across the Ægean. At this time Croesus was the master and tribute-exactor of the Asiatic Greeks, whose contingents seem to have formed part of his army for the expedition now contemplated; an army consisting principally, not of native Lydians, but of foreigners.

The river Halys formed the boundary at this time between the Median and Lydian empires: and Croesus, marching across that river into the territory of the Syrians or Assyrians of Cappadocia, took the city of Pteria, with many of its surrounding dependencies, inflicting damage and destruction upon these distant subjects of Ekbatana. Cyrus lost no time in bringing an army to their defence considerably larger than that of Croesus; trying at the same time, though unsuccessfully, to prevail on the Ionians to revolt from him. A bloody battle took place between the two armies, but with indecisive result: after which Croesus, seeing that he could not hope to accomplish more with his forces as they stood, thought it wise to return to his capital, and collect a larger army for the next campaign. Immediately on reaching Sardis he despatched envoys to Labynetus king of Babylon; to Amasis, king of Egypt; to the Lacedæmonians, and to other allies; calling upon all of them to send auxiliaries to Sardis during the course of the fifth month. In the mean time he dismissed all the foreign troops who had followed him into Cappadocia.

Had these allies appeared, the war might perhaps have been prosecuted with success. And on the part of the Lacedæmonians, at least, there was no tardiness; for their ships were ready and their troops almost on board, when the unexpected news reached them that Croesus was already ruined. Cyrus had forseen and forestalled the defensive plan of his enemy. Pushing on with his army to Sardis without delay, he obliged the Lydian prince to give battle with his own unassisted subjects. The open and spacious plain before that town was highly favorable to Lydian cavalry, which at that time (Herodotus tells us) was superior to the Persian. But Cyrus, employing a strategem whereby this cavalry was rendered unavailable, placed in front of his line the baggage camels, which the Lydian horses could not endure either to smell or to behold. The horsemen of Croesus were thus obliged to dismount; nevertheless they fought bravely on foot, and were not driven into the town till after a sanguinary combat.

Though confined within the walls of his capital, Croesus had still good reason for hoping to hold out until the arrival of his allies, to whom he sent pressing envoys of acceleration. For Sardis was considered impregnable—and one assault had already been repulsed, and the Persians would have been reduced to the slow process of blockade. But on the fourteenth day of the siege, accident did for the besiegers that which they could not have accomplished either by skill or force. Sardis was situated on an outlying peak of the northern side of Tmolus; it was well fortified everywhere except toward the mountain; and on that side the rock was so precipitous and inaccessible, that fortifications were thought unnecessary, nor did the inhabitants believe assault to be possible in that quarter. But Hyroeades, a Persian soldier, having accidentally seen one of the garrison descending this precipi tous rock to pick up his helmet which had rolled down, watched his opportunity, tried to climb up, and found it not impracticable; others followed his example, the stronghold was thus seized first, and the whole city speedily taken by storm.

Cyrus had given especial orders to spare the life of Croesus, who was accordingly made prisoner. But preparations were made for a solemn and terrible spectacle; the captive king was destined to be burned in chains, together with fourteen Lydian youths, on a vast pile of wood. We are even told that the pile was already kindled and the victim beyond the reach of human aid, when Apollo sent a miraculous rain to preserve him. As to the general fact of supernatural interposition, in one way or another,

Herodotus and Ctesias both agree, though they described differently the particular miracles wrought. It is certain that Croesus, after some time, was released and well treated by his conqueror, and lived to become the confidential adviser of the latter as well as of his son Cambyses: Ctesias also acquaints us that a considerable town and territory near Ekbatana, called Barene, was assigned to him, according to a practice which we shall find not infrequent with the Persian kings.

The prudent counsel and remarks as to the relations between Persians and Lydians, whereby Croesus is said by Herodotus to have first earned this favorable treatment, are hardly worth repeating; but the indignant remonstrance sent by Croesus to the Delphian god is too characteristic to be passed over. He obtained permission from Cyrus to lay upon the holy pavement of the Delphian temple the chains with which he had at first been bound. The Lydian envoys were instructed, after exhibiting to the god these humiliating memorials, to ask whether it was his custom to deceive his benefactors, and whether he was not ashamed to have encouraged the king of Lydia in an enterprise so disastrous? The god, condescending to justify himself by the lips of the priestess, replied: "Not even a god can escape his destiny. Croesus has suffered for the sin of his fifth ancestor (Gyges), who, conspiring with a woman, slew his master and wrongfully seized the sceptre. Apollo employed all his influence with the Moeræ (Fates) to obtain that this sin might be expiated by the children of Croesus, and not by Croesus himself; but the Moeræ would grant nothing more than a postponement of the judgment for three years. Let Croesus know that Apollo has thus procured for him a reign three years longer than his original destiny, after having tried in vain to rescue him altogether. Moreover he sent that rain which at the critical moment extinguished the burning pile. Nor has Croesus any right to complain of the prophecy by which he was encouraged to enter on the war; for when the god told him that he would subvert *a great* empire, *it was his duty to have again inquired which empire the god* meant; and if he neither understood the meaning, nor chose to ask for information, he has himself to blame for the result. Besides, Croesus neglected the warning given to him about the acquisition of the Median kingdom by a mule: Cyrus was that mule—son of a Median mother of royal breed, by a Persian father at once of different race and of lower position."

This triumphant justification extorted even from Croesus himself a full confession that the sin lay with him, and not with the god. It certainly illustrates in a remarkable manner the theological ideas of the time. It shows us how much, in the mind of Herodotus, the facts of the centuries preceding his own, unrecorded as they were by any contemporary authority, tended to cast themselves into a sort of religious drama; the threads of the historical web being in part put together, in part originally spun, for the purpose of setting forth the religious sentiment and doctrine woven in as a pattern. The Pythian priestess predicts to Gyges that the crime which he had committed in assassinating his master would be expiated by his fifth descendant, though, as Herodotus tells us, no one took any notice of this prophecy until it was at last fulfilled: we see thus the history of the first Mermnad king is made up after the catastrophe of the last. There was something in the main facts of the history of Croesus profoundly striking to the Greek mind, a king at the summit of wealth and power—pious in the extreme and munificent toward the gods—the first destroyer of Hellenic liberty in Asia—then precipitated, at once and on a sudden, into the abyss of ruin. The sin of the first parent helped much toward the solution of this perplexing problem, as well as to exalt the credit of the oracle, when made to assume the shape of an unnoticed prophecy. In the affecting story of Solon and Croesus, the Lydian king is punished with an acute domestic affliction because he thought himself the happiest of mankind—the gods not suffering any one to be arrogant except themselves; and the warning of Solon is made to recur to Croesus after he has become the prisoner of Cyrus, in the narrative of Herodotus. To the same vein of thought belongs the story, just recounted, of the relations of Croesus with the Delphian oracle. An account is provided, satisfactory to the religious feelings of the Greeks, how and why he was ruined—but nothing less than the overruling and omnipotent Moeræ could be invoked to explain so stupendous a result. It is rarely that these supreme goddesses—or hyper-goddesses, since the gods themselves must submit to them—are brought into such distinct light and action. Usually they are kept in the dark, or are left to be understood as the unseen stumbling block in cases of extreme incomprehensibility; and it is difficult clearly to determine (as in the case of some complicated political constitutions) where the Greeks conceived sovereign power to reside, in respect to the government of the world. But here the sovereignity of the Moeræ, and the subordinate agency of the gods, are unequivocally set forth. The gods are still extremely powerful, because the Moeræ comply with their requests up to a certain point, not thinking it proper to be wholly inexorable; but their compliance is carried no farther than they themselves choose; nor would they, even in deference to

Apollo, alter the original sentence of punishment for the sin of Gyges in the person of his fifth descendant—sentence, moreover, which Apollo himself had formerly prophesied shortly after the sin was committed, so that, if the Moeræ had listened to his intercession on behalf of Croesus, his own prophetic credit would have been endangered. Their unalterable resolution has predetermined the ruin of Croesus, and the grandeur of the event is manifested by the circumstance that even Apollo himself cannot prevail upon them to alter it, or to grant more than a three years' respite. The religious element must here be viewed as giving the form, the historical element as giving the matter only, and not the whole matter, of the story. These two elements will be found conjoined more or less throughout most of the history of Herodotus, though as we descend to later times, we shall find the latter element in constantly increasing proportion. His conception of history is extremely different from that of Thucydides, who lays down to himself the true scheme and purpose of the historian, common to him with the philosopher—to recount and interpret the past, as a rational aid toward pre-vision of the future.

*

In the short abstract which we now possess of the lost work of Ctesias, no mention appears of the important conquest of Babylon. His narrative, indeed, as far as the abstract enables us to follow it, diverges materially from that of Herodotus, and must have been founded on data altogether different.

"I shall mention (says Herodotus) these conquests which gave Cyrus most trouble, and are most memorable: after he had subdued all the rest of the continent, he attacked the Assyrians." Those who recollect the description of Babylon and its surrounding territory, will not be surprised to learn that the capture of it gave the Persian aggressor much trouble. Their only surprise will be, how it could ever have been taken at all—or indeed how a hostile army could have even reached it. Herodotus informs us that the Babylonian queen Nitocris (mother of that very Labynetus who was king when Cyrus attacked the place) apprehensive of invasion from the Medes after their capture of Nineveh, had executed many laborious works near the Euphrates for the purpose of obstructing their approach. Moreover there existed what was called the wall of Media (probably built by her, but certainly built prior to the Persian conquest), one hundred feet high and twenty feet thick, across the entire space of seventy-five miles which joined the Tigris with one of the canals of the Euphrates: while the canals themselves, as we may see by the march of the ten thousand Greeks after the battle of Cunaxa, presented means of defence altogether insuperable by a rude army such as that of the Persians. On the east, the territory of Babylonia was defended by the Tigris, which cannot be forded lower than the ancient Nineveh or the modern Mosul. In addition to these ramparts, natural as well as artificial, to protect the territory—populous, cultivated, productive, and offering every motive to its inhabitants to resist even the entrance of an enemy—we are told that the Babylonians were so thoroughly prepared for the inroad of Cyrus that they had accumulated within their walls a store of provisions for many years. Strange as it may seem, we must suppose that the king of Babylon, after all the cost and labor spent in providing defences for the territory, voluntarily neglected to avail himself of them, suffered the invader to tread down the fertile Babylonia without resistance, and merely drew out the citizens to oppose him when he arrived under the walls of the city—if the statement of Herodotus is correct. And we may illustrate this unaccountable omission by that which we know to have happened in the march of the younger Cyrus to Cunuxa against his brother Artaxerxes Mnemon. The latter had caused to be dug, expressly in preparation for this invasion, a broad and deep ditch (thirty feet wide and eight feet deep) from the wall of Media to the river Euphrates, a distance of twelve parasangs or forty-five English miles, leaving only a passage of twenty feet broad close alongside of the river. Yet when the invading army arrived at this important pass, they found not a man there to defend it, and all of them marched without resistance through the narrow inlet. Cyrus the younger, who had up to that moment felt assured that his brother would fight, now supposed that he had given up the idea of defending Babylon: instead of which, two days afterward, Artaxerxes attacked him on an open plain of ground where there was no advantage of position on either side; though the invaders were taken rather unawares in consequence of their extreme confidence arising from recent unopposed entrance within the artificial ditch. This anecdote is the more valuable as an illustration, because all its circumstances are transmitted to us by a discerning eye-witness. And both the two incidents here brought into comparison demonstrate the recklessness, changefulness, and incapacity of calculation belonging to the Asiatic mind of that day—as well as the great command of hands possessed by these kings, and their prodigal waste of human labor. Vast walls and deep ditches are an inestimable aid to a brave and well-commanded garrison; but they cannot be made entirely to supply the want of bravery and intelligence.

*

In whatever manner the difficulties of approaching Babylon may have been overcome, the fact that they were overcome by Cyrus is certain. On first setting out for this conquest, he was about to cross the river Gyndes (one of the affluents from the east which joins the Tigris near the modern Bagdad, and along which lay the high road crossing the pass of Mount Zagros from Babylon to Ekbatana) when one of the sacred white horses, which accompanied him, entered the river in pure wantonness and tried to cross it by himself. The Gyndes resented this insult and the horse was drowned: upon which Cyrus swore in his wrath that he would so break the strength of the river as that women in future should pass it without wetting their knees. Accordingly he employed his entire army, during the whole summer season, in digging three hundred and sixty artificial channels to disseminate the unit of the stream. Such, according to Herodotus, was the incident which postponed for one year the fall of the great Babylon. But in the next spring Cyrus and his army were before the walls, after having defeated and driven in the population who came out to fight. These walls were artificial mountains (three hundred feet high, seventy-five feet thick, and forming a square of fifteen miles to each side), within which the besieged defied attack, and even blockade, having previously stored up several years' provision. Through the midst of the town, however, flowed the Euphrates. That river which had been so laboriously trained to serve for protection, trade and sustenance to the Babylonians, was now made the avenue of their ruin. Having left a detachment of his army at the two points where the Euphrates enters and quits the city, Cyrus retired with the remainder to the higher part of its course, where an ancient Babylonian queen had prepared one of the great lateral reservoirs for carrying off in case of need the superfluity of its water. Near this point Cyrus caused another reservoir and another canal of communication to be dug, by means of which he drew off the water of the Euphrates to such a degree it became not above the height of a man's thigh. The period chosen was that of a great Babylonian festival, when the whole population were engaged in amusement and revelry. The Persian troops left near the town, watching their opportunity, entered from both sides along the bed of the river, and took it by surprise with scarcely any resistance. At no other time, except during a festival, could they have done this (says Herodotus) had the river been ever so low, for both banks throughout the whole length of the town were provided with quays, with continuous walls, and with gates at the end of every street which led down to the river at right angles so that if the population had not been disqualified by the influences of the moment, they would have caught the assailants in the bed of the river "as in a trap," and overwhelmed them from the walls alongside. Within a square of fifteen miles to each side, we are not surprised to hear that both the extremities were already in the power of the besiegers before the central population heard of it, and while they were yet absorbed in unconscious festivity.

Such is the account given by Herodotus of the circumstances which placed Babylon—the greatest city of Western Asia—in the power of the Persians. To what extent the information communicated to him was incorrect or exaggerated, we cannot now decide. The way in which the city was treated would lead us to suppose that its acquisition cannot have cost the conqueror either much time or much loss. Cyrus comes into the list as king of Babylon, and the inhabitants with their whole territory become tributary to the Persians, forming the richest satrapy in the empire; but we do not hear that the people were otherwise ill-used, and it is certain that the vast walls and gates were left untouched. This was very different from the way in which the Medes had treated Nineveh, which seems to have been ruined and for a long time absolutely uninhabited, though reoccupied on a reduced scale under the Parthian empire; and very different also from the way in which Babylon itself was treated twenty years afterward by Darius, when reconquered after a revolt.

Chapter 3
Alexander the Great[5].

Alexander the Great, son of Philip of Macedon and Olympias, daughter of Neoptolemus of Epirus, was born at Pella, 356 B.C. His mind was formed chiefly by Aristotle, who instructed him in every branch of human learning, especially in the art of government. Alexander was sixteen years of age when his father marched against Byzantium, and left the government in his hands during his absence. Two years afterward, he displayed singular courage at the battle of Chæronea (338 B.C.), where he overthrew the Sacred Band of the Thebans. "My son," said Philip, as he embraced him after the conflict, "seek for thyself another kingdom, for that which I leave is too small

---

[5] By Clarence Cook

for thee." The father and son quarrelled, however, when the former divorced Olympias. Alexander took part with his mother, and fled to Epirus, to escape his father's vengeance; but receiving his pardon soon afterward, he returned, and accompanied him in an expedition against the Triballi, when he saved his life on the field. Philip, being appointed generalissimo of the Greeks, was preparing for a war with Persia, when he was assassinated (336 B.C.), and Alexander, not yet twenty years of age, ascended the throne.

After punishing his father's murderers, he marched on Corinth, and in a general assembly of the Greeks he caused himself to be appointed to the command of the forces against Persia. On his return to Macedon, he found the Illyrians and Triballi up in arms, whereupon he forced his way through Thrace, and was everywhere victorious. But now the Thebans had been induced, by a report of his death, to take up arms, and the Athenians, stimulated by the eloquence of Demosthenes, were preparing to join them. To prevent this coalition, Alexander rapidly marched against Thebes, which, refusing to surrender, was conquered and razed to the ground. Six thousand of the inhabitants were slain, and 30,000 sold into slavery; the house and descendants of the poet Pindar alone being spared. This severity struck terror into all Greece. The Athenians were treated with more leniency.

Alexander, having appointed Antipater his deputy in Europe, now prepared to prosecute the war with Persia. He crossed the Hellespont in the spring of 334 B.C. with 30,000 foot and 5,000 horse, attacked the Persian satraps at the River Granicus, and gained a complete victory, overthrowing the son-in-law of their king Darius with his own lance. As a result of the battle, most of the cities of Asia Minor at once opened their gates to the conqueror.

Alexander restored democracy in all the Greek cities; and as he passed through Gordium, cut the Gordian-knot, which none should loose but the ruler of Asia. During a dangerous illness at Tarsus, brought on by bathing in the Cydnus, he received a letter insinuating that Philip, his physician, had been bribed by Darius to poison him. Alexander handed the letter to Philip, and at the same time swallowed the draught which the latter had prepared. As soon as he recovered, he advanced toward the defiles of Cilicia, in which Darius had stationed himself with an army of 600,000 men.

He arrived in November, 333 B.C., in the neighborhood of Issus, where, on the narrow plain between the mountains and the sea, the unwieldy masses of the Persians were thrown into confusion by the charge of the Macedonians, and fled in terror. On the left wing, 30,000 Greek mercenaries held out longer, but they, too, were at length compelled to yield. All the treasures as well as the family of Darius fell into the hands of the conqueror, who treated them with the greatest magnanimity. Overtures for peace, made by Darius on the basis of surrendering to Alexander all Asia west of the Euphrates, were rejected.

Alexander now turned toward Syria and Phœnicia. He occupied Damascus, where he found princely treasures, and secured to himself all the cities along the shores of the Mediterranean. Tyre, confident in its strong position, resisted him, but was conquered and destroyed, after seven months of incredible exertion (332 B.C.) Thence he marched victoriously through Palestine, where all the cities submitted to him except

Gaza; it shared the same fate as Tyre. Egypt, weary of the Persian yoke, welcomed him as a deliverer; and in order to strengthen his dominion here, he restored all the old customs and religious institutions of the country, and founded Alexandria in the beginning of 331 B.C. Thence he marched through the Libyan Desert, in order to consult the oracle of Ammon, whose priest saluted him as a son of Zeus; and he returned with the conviction that he was indeed a god.

He then again set out to meet Darius; in October, 331 B.C., a great battle was fought on the plain stretching eastward to Arbela. Notwithstanding the immense superiority of his adversary, who had collected a new army of more than a million men, Alexander was not for a moment doubtful of victory. Heading the cavalry himself, he rushed on the Persians, and put them to flight; then hastened to the assistance of his left wing, which, in the meanwhile, had been sorely pressed. He was anxious to make Darius a prisoner, but Darius escaped on horseback, leaving his baggage and all his treasures a prey to the conqueror. Babylon and Susa, the treasure-houses of the East, opened their gates to Alexander, who next marched toward Persepolis, the capital of Persia, which he entered in triumph.

The marvellous successes of Alexander now began to dazzle his judgment and to inflame his passions. He became a slave to debauchery, and his caprices were as cruel as they were ungrateful. In a fit of drunkenness, and at the instigation of Thaïs, an Athenian courtesan, he set fire to Persepolis, the wonder of the world, and reduced it to a heap of ashes; then, ashamed of the deed, he set out with his cavalry in pursuit of Darius. Learning that Bessus, the Bactrian satrap, held him a prisoner, he hastened his march, in the hope of saving him, but he found him mortally wounded (330 B.C.). He mourned over his fallen enemy, and caused him to be buried with all the customary honors, while he hunted down Bessus, who himself aspired to the throne, chasing him over the Oxus to Sogdiana (Bokhara).

Having discovered a conspiracy in which the son of Parmenio was implicated, he put both father and son to death, though Parmenio himself was innocent of any knowledge of the affair. This cruel injustice excited universal displeasure. In 329 he penetrated to the farthest known limits of Northern Asia, and overthrew the Scythians on the banks of the Jaxartes. In the following year he subdued the whole of Sogdiana, and married Roxana, whom he had taken prisoner. She was the daughter of Oxyartes, one of the enemy's captains, and was said to be the fairest of all the virgins of Asia. The murder of his foster-brother, Clitus, in a drunken brawl, was followed, in 327 B.C., by the discovery of a fresh conspiracy, in which Callisthenes, a nephew of Aristotle, was falsely implicated. For challenging Alexander's divinity, he was cruelly tortured and hanged.

In 327 B.C., proceeding to the conquest of India, hitherto known only by name, Alexander crossed the Indus near to the modern Attock, and pursued his way under the guidance of a native prince to the Hydaspes (Jhelum). He there was opposed by Porus, another native prince, whom he overthrew after a bloody contest, and there he lost his charger Bucephalus; thence he marched as lord of the country, through the Punjab, establishing Greek colonies. He then wished to advance to the Ganges, but the general murmuring of his troops obliged him, at the Hyphasis (modern Sutlej), to commence his retreat. On regaining the Hydaspes, he built a fleet, and sent one division of his army in it down the river, while the other followed along the banks, fighting its way through successive Indian armies. At length, having reached the ocean, he ordered Nearchus, the commander of the fleet, to sail thence to the Persian Gulf, while he himself struck inland with one division of his army, in order to return home through Gedrosia (Beluchistan). During this march his forces suffered fearfully from want of food and water. Of all the troops which had set out with Alexander, little more than a fourth part arrived with him in Persia (325 B.C.).

At Susa he married Stateira, the daughter of Darius, and he bestowed presents on those Macedonians (some ten thousand in number) who had married Persian women, his design being to unite the two nations. He also distributed liberal rewards among his soldiers. Soon afterward he was deprived, by death, of his favorite Hephestion. His grief was unbounded, and he interred the dead man with kingly honors. As he was returning from Ecbatana to Babylon, it is said that the Magi foretold that the latter city would prove fatal to him; but he despised their warnings. On the way, he was met by ambassadors from all parts of the world—Libya, Italy, Carthage, Greece, the Scythians, Celts, and Iberians.

At Babylon he was busy with gigantic plans for the future, both of conquest and civilization, when he was suddenly taken ill after a banquet, and died eleven days later, 323 B.C., in the thirty-second year of his age, and the thirteenth of his reign. His body was deposited in a golden coffin at Alexandria, by Ptolemæus, and divine honors were paid to him, not only in Egypt, but in other countries. He had appointed no heir to his immense dominions; but to the question of his friends, "Who should inherit them?" he replied, "The most worthy." After many disturbances, his generals recognized as Kings the weak-minded Aridæus—a son of Philip by Philinna, the dancer—and Alexander's posthumous son by Roxana, Alexander Ægus, while they shared the provinces among themselves, assuming the title of satraps. Perdiccas, to whom Alexander had, on his death-bed, delivered his ring, became guardian of the kings during their minority. The empire of Alexander soon broke up, and his dominions were divided among his generals.

Alexander was more than a conqueror. He diffused the language and civilization of Greece wherever victory led him, and planted Greek kingdoms in Asia, which continued to exist for some centuries. At the very time of his death, he was engaged in devising plans for the drainage of the unhealthy marshes around Babylon, and a better irrigation of the extensive plains. It is even supposed that the fever which he caught there, rather than his famous drinking-bout, was the real cause of his death. To Alexander, the ancient world owed a vast increase of its knowledge in geography, natural history, etc. He taught Europeans the road to India, and gave them the first glimpses of that magnificence and splendor which has dazzled and captivated their imagination for more than two thousand years. See Freeman's "Historical Essays" (2d series, 1873), and Mahaffy's "Alexander's Empire" (1887).

The wonderful element in the campaigns of Alexander, and his tragical death at the height of his power, threw a rare romantic interest around his figure. It is ever the fate of a great name to be enshrined in fable, and Alexander soon became the hero of romantic story, scarcely more wonderful than the actual, but growing from age to age with the mythopœic spirit which can work as freely in fact as fiction.

The earliest form of the story which we know is the great romance connected with the name of Callisthenes, which, under the influence of the living popular tradition, arose in Egypt about 200 A.D., and was carried through Latin translations to the West, through Armenian and Syriac versions to the East. It became widely popular during the middle ages, and was worked into poetic form by many writers in French and German. Alberich of Besançon wrote in Middle High German an epic on the subject in the first half of the twelfth century, which was the basis of the German "Pfaffe" Lamprecht's "Alexanderbuch," also of the twelfth century. The French poets Lambert li Court and Alexandre de Bernay composed, between 1180 and 1190, a romance of Alexander, the twelve-syllable metre of which gave rise to the name Alexandrines.

The German poem of Rudolf of Ems was based on the Latin epic of Walter of Châtillon, about 1200, which became henceforward the prevailing form of the story. In contrast with it is the thirteenth century Old English epic of Alexander, based on the Callisthenes version. The story appears also in the East, worked up in conjunction with myths of other nationalities, especially the Persian. It appears in Firdusi, and among later writers, in Nizami. From the Persians both the substance of the story and its form in poetical treatment have extended to Turks and other Mohammedans, who have interpreted Alexander as the Dsulkarnein ('two horned') of the Koran, and to the Hindus, which last had preserved no independent traditions of Alexander.

Alexander and his Horse Bucephalus[6].

One day King Philip bought a fine horse called Bucephalus. He was a noble animal, and the king paid a very high price for him. But he was wild and savage, and no man could mount him, or do anything at all with him.

They tried to whip him, but that only made him worse. At last the king bade his servants take him away.

"It is a pity to ruin so fine a horse as that," said Alexander, the king's young son. "Those men do not know how to treat him."

"Perhaps you can do better than they," said his father scornfully.

"I know," said Alexander, "that, if you would only give me leave to try, I could manage this horse better than anyone else."

---

[6] cf James Baldwin, in *Fifty Famous Stories Retold*.

"And if you fail to do so, what then?" asked Philip.

"I will pay you the price of the horse" said the lad.

While everybody was laughing, Alexander ran up to Bucephalus, and turned his head toward the sun. He had noticed that the horse was afraid of his own shadow.

He then spoke gently to the horse, and patted him with his hand. When he had quieted him a little, he made a quick spring, and leaped upon the horse's back.

Everybody expected to see the boy killed outright. But he kept his place, and let the horse run as fast as he would. By and by, when Bucephalus had become tired, Alexander reined him in, and rode back to the place where his father was standing.

All the men who were there shouted when they saw that the boy had proved himself to be the master of the horse.

He leaped to the ground, and his father ran and kissed him.

"My son," said the king, "Macedon is too small a place for you. You must seek a larger kingdom that will be worthy of you."

After that, Alexander and Bucephalus were the best of friends. They were said to be always together, for when one of them was seen, the other was sure to be not far away. But the horse would never allow anyone to mount him but his master.

Alexander became the most famous king and warrior that was ever known; and for that reason he is always called Alexander the Great. Bucephalus carried him through many countries and in many fierce battles, and more than once did he save his master's life.

The Empire of Alexander the Great[7].

From 431 to 404 B.C. the Peloponnesian War wasted Greece. Meanwhile to the north of Greece, the kindred country of Macedonia was rising slowly to power and civilization. The Macedonians spoke a language closely akin to Greek, and on several occasions Macedonian competitors had taken part in the Olympic games. In 359 B.C. a man of very great abilities and ambition became king of this little country—Philip. Philip had previously been a hostage in Greece; he had had a thoroughly Greek education and he was probably aware of the ideas of Herodotus—which had also been developed by the philosopher Isocrates—of a possible conquest of Asia by a consolidated Greece.

---

[7].cf H. G. Wells, in *A Short History of the World.*

He set himself first to extend and organize his own realm and to remodel his army. For a thousand years now the charging horse-chariot had been the decisive factor in battles, that and the close-fighting infantry. Mounted horsemen had also fought, but as a cloud of skirmishers, individually and without discipline. Philip made his infantry fight in a closely packed mass, the Macedonian phalanx, and he trained his mounted gentlemen, the knights or companions, to fight in formation and so invented cavalry. The master move in most of his battles and in the battles of his son Alexander was a cavalry charge. The phalanx *held* the enemy infantry in front while the cavalry swept away the enemy horse on his wings and poured in on the flank and rear of his infantry. Chariots were disabled by bowmen, who shot the horses.

With this new army Philip extended his frontiers through Thessaly to Greece; and the battle of Chæronia (338 B.C.), fought against Athens and her allies, put all Greece at his feet. At last the dream of Herodotus was bearing fruit. A congress of all the Greek states appointed Philip captain-general of the Græco- Macedonian confederacy against Persia, and in 336 B.C. his advanced guard crossed into Asia upon this long premeditated adventure. But he never followed it. He was assassinated; it is believed at the instigation of his queen Olympias, Alexander's mother. She was jealous because Philip had married a second wife.

But Philip had taken unusual pains with his son's education. He had not only secured Aristotle, the greatest philosopher in the world, as this boy's tutor, but he had shared his ideas with him and thrust military experience upon him. At Chæronia Alexander, who was then only eighteen years old, had been in command of the cavalry. And so it was possible for this young man, who was still only twenty years old at the time of his accession, to take up his father's task at once and to proceed successfully with the Persian adventure.

In 334 B.C.—for two years were needed to establish and confirm his position in Macedonia and Greece—he crossed into Asia, defeated a not very much bigger Persian army at the battle of the Granicus and captured a number of cities in Asia Minor. He kept along the sea-coast. It was necessary for him to reduce and garrison all the coast towns as he advanced because the Persians had control of the fleets of Tyre and Sidon and so had command of the sea. Had he left a hostile port in his rear the Persians might have landed forces to raid his communications and cut him off. At Issus (333 B.C.) he met and smashed a vast conglomerate host under Darius III. Like the host of Xerxes that had crossed the Dardanelles a century and a half before, it was an incoherent accumulation of contingents and it was encumbered with a multitude of court officials, the harem of Darius and many camp followers. Sidon surrendered to Alexander but Tyre resisted obstinately. Finally that great city was stormed and plundered and destroyed. Gaza also was stormed, and towards the end of 332 B.C. the conqueror entered Egypt and took over its rule from the Persians.

At Alexandretta and at Alexandria in Egypt he built great cities, accessible from the land and so incapable of revolt. To these the trade of the Phœnician cities was diverted. The Phœnicians of the western Mediterranean suddenly disappear from history—and as immediately the Jews of Alexandria and the other new trading cities created by Alexander appear.

In 331 B.C. Alexander marched out of Egypt upon Babylon as Thothmes and Rameses and Necho had done before him. But he marched by way of Tyre. At Arbela near the ruins of Nineveh, which was already a forgotten city, he met Darius and fought the decisive battle of the war. The Persian chariot charge failed, a Macedonian cavalry charge broke up the great composite host and the phalanx completed the victory. Darius led the retreat. He made no further attempt to resist the invader but fled northward into the country of the Medes. Alexander marched on to Babylon, still prosperous and important, and then to Susa and Persepolis. There after a drunken festival he burnt down the palace of Darius, the king of kings.

Thence Alexander presently made a military parade of central Asia, going to the utmost bounds of the Persian empire. At first he turned northward. Darius was pursued; and he was overtaken at dawn dying in his chariot, having been murdered by his own people. He was still living when the foremost Greeks reached him. Alexander came up to find him dead. Alexander skirted the Caspian Sea, he went up into the mountains of western Turkestan, he came down by Herat (which he founded) and Cabul and the Khyber Pass into India. He fought a great battle on the Indus with an Indian king, Porus, and here the Macedonian troops met elephants for the first time and defeated them. Finally he built himself ships, sailed down to the mouth of the Indus, and marched back by the coast of Beluchistan, reaching Susa again in 324 B.C. after an absence of six years. He then prepared to consolidate and organize this vast empire he had won. He sought to win over his new subjects. He assumed the robes and tiara of a Persian monarch, and this roused the jealousy of his Macedonian commanders. He had much trouble with them. He arranged a number of marriages between these Macedonian officers and Persian and Babylonian women: the "Marriage of the East and West." He never lived to effect the consolidation he had planned. A fever seized him after a drinking bout in Babylon and he died in 323 B.C.

Immediately this vast dominion fell to pieces. One of his generals, Seleucus, retained most of the old Persian empire from the Indus to Ephesus; another, Ptolemy, seized Egypt, and Antigonus secured Macedonia. The rest of the empire remained unstable, passing under the control of a succession of local adventurers. Barbarian raids began from the north and grew in scope and intensity. Until at last, as we shall tell, a new power, the power of the Roman republic, came out of the west to subjugate one fragment after another and weld them together into a new and more enduring empire.

9 782384 690275